Go Ba

Amy woke up.
"Mom, Mom! There's a
dinosaur outside," said Amy.

"Go to sleep," said Mom.

"Dad, Dad!" There's a
dinosaur outside," said Amy.

4

"Go to sleep," said Dad.

5

"Sam, Sam! There's a
dinosaur outside," said Amy.

"Go to sleep," said Sam.

"There really *is*
a dinosaur outside!"
screamed Amy.

8

Mom came running.
Dad came running.
Sam came running.

"Shh, shh, shh," said Mom.

"It's only the garbage truck."

So Amy went to sleep.